HIS MAJESTY'S SPEECHES

HIS MAJESTY THE KING

*Vandyk*

# HIS
# MAJESTY'S
# SPEECHES

THE
RECORD OF
THE SILVER JUBILEE

*of*

HIS MOST GRACIOUS MAJESTY
KING GEORGE
THE FIFTH

1935

HER MAJESTY THE QUEEN

*Vandyk*

# A
# PRAYER FOR
# THE KING'S MAJESTY

*O God, whose mercy is our state,*
*Whose realms are children in Thy hand,*
*Who willed that, in the years of Fate,*
*Thy servant George should rule this land,*

*We thank Thee, that the years of strife*
*Have changed to peace, and for this thing*
*That Thou hast given him length of life*
*Under Thy hand to be our King.*

*O God, vouchsafe him many years*
*With all the world as England's friend*
*And England bright among her peers*
*With wisdom that can never end.*

JOHN MASEFIELD, *Poet Laureate.*

By His Majesty's gracious permission, this book is published by King George's Jubilee Trust, to which the entire proceeds from its sale will be devoted. I feel sure that many people will wish to possess this record of a memorable occasion, thereby contributing to the Trust which I have inaugurated as a tribute to the King and Queen on behalf of the rising generation.

EDWARD P.

# CONTENTS

A Prayer for The King's Majesty . . . Page 5

Introduction . . . . . . Page 8

The Thanksgiving Service . . . . Page 11

The Broadcast Messages from His Majesty's
Overseas Dominions . . . . Page 14

The Prime Minister's Message . . . Page 18

HIS MAJESTY'S MESSAGE TO HIS PEOPLES Page 21

His Majesty's Reception of Representatives of
the Corps Diplomatique and of His Majesty's
Overseas Dominions . . . . Page 23

HIS MAJESTY'S REPLY TO HIS EXCELLENCY
THE BRAZILIAN AMBASSADOR . . Page 25

The Addresses from His Majesty's Overseas
Dominions . . . . . . Page 27

HIS MAJESTY'S REPLY TO THE REPRESENTA-
TIVES OF THE OVERSEAS DOMINIONS . Page 37

The Presentation of Addresses to His Majesty by
His Lords and Commons . . . Page 41

HIS MAJESTY'S REPLY TO THE ADDRESSES
FROM HIS LORDS AND COMMONS . . Page 49

HIS MAJESTY'S MESSAGE TO THE CHILDREN
OF LONDON . . . . . . Page 53

The Jubilee Celebrations . . . . Page 54

King George's Jubilee Trust . . . . Page 55

# INTRODUCTION

TO all who witnessed the Empire's tribute to Their
Majesties on their Silver Jubilee and to those all
over the world who joined in spirit in that tribute,
this book is offered with a twofold purpose.

The spoken word is with us only for the moment;
the printed word endures. In these pages, as a record
of an occasion that will remain for ever in our minds, we
have the memorable words of His Majesty and the
messages from all parts of his Empire, to which they are
the reply.

Every corner of the earth has joined in heartfelt
congratulations on the twenty-five years' devoted service
that preceded the unforgettable scenes of the Silver
Jubilee. Everywhere is evident the desire that the gratitude of our nation to its King and Queen be given
permanent expression.

It is for this that His Majesty has graciously approved
the formation of King George's Jubilee Trust, devoted
to the welfare of the rising generation. No vital issue
in our national life to-day could have provided a more
fitting purpose to which to dedicate this Thank-offering.

Each person who secures this record of the Silver
Jubilee thereby contributes a share to this yet more lasting
commemoration of their love and loyalty.

Among all the recollections of the Jubilee Year of
1935 that Their Majesties will treasure, surely none
will give them more happiness than this great national
Trust inaugurated on behalf of Britain's youth.

The arrival of Their Majesties at St. Paul's Cathedral, on May the Sixth, 1935.

The scene in St. Paul's Cathedral during the Thanksgiving Service.

# THE
# THANKSGIVING SERVICE

## TO COMMEMORATE THE TWENTY-FIFTH ANNIVERSARY OF HIS MAJESTY'S ACCESSION TO THE THRONE

### *At St. Paul's Cathedral*

#### MAY 6th, 1935

ON Monday, May the Sixth, 1935, His Majesty King George the Fifth and Her Majesty Queen Mary, on the occasion of the Twenty-Fifth anniversary of His Majesty's Accession to the Throne, attended a Thanksgiving Service at St. Paul's Cathedral, and drove in State through London amidst scenes of unprecedented enthusiasm.

His Majesty's Carriage Procession was escorted by a Sovereign's Escort of The Life Guards. It was preceded by the Carriage Procession of H.R.H. the Prince of Wales and that of H.R.H. the Duke of York, a Car Procession of Members of the Royal Family other than those in the Royal Carriage Processions, the Carriage Procession of The Lord High Chancellor, that of The Speaker of the House of Commons and that of the Prime Minister of Great Britain and the Dominion Prime Ministers.

On arrival at Temple Bar, His Majesty was presented with the Pearl Sword of the City of London by the Right Honourable, the Lord Mayor of London, who then preceded His Majesty's Carriage Procession to St. Paul's Cathedral. The Thanksgiving Service commenced at 11.30 a.m. Below is given the address delivered by The Lord Archbishop of Canterbury.

## THE ARCHBISHOP OF CANTERBURY'S ADDRESS

Twenty-five years have passed since the reign of our beloved Sovereign began. Looking back upon them we realize, as he of all men must, that more perhaps than in any previous period of our long history they have been years of almost unbroken anxiety and strain. They began in an atmosphere of embittered party strife. Into the midst of them came suddenly the fiercest ordeal which the nation has ever been summoned to face. Since then have followed years of toilsome effort in the midst of a world restless, bewildered, broken by the shock of war, to revive the trade and industry on which the lives of multitudes depend and to find the bases of a settled peace. Yet beneath the troubled surface there has been in the life of our nation the deep underflow of a spirit of unity, confidence, and steadfast strength. That spirit has found a centre in the Throne. Elsewhere ancient monarchies have been swept away by the storms of revolution. Here the Throne has been established in ever stronger security.

Across the seas during these 25 years the attainment of full nationhood by the great Dominions has been acknowledged. The Empire has become a Fellowship of self-governing peoples. Yet their freedom has not lessened but strengthened loyalty to the one Commonwealth; and it is in the one Throne that they find the symbol and bond of their unity.

It may be, that, by the mere force of circumstances or of sentiment, the Throne itself would have been accepted by the people of this realm and the nations of the Empire as the centre of their unity. What is certain is that the personality of the King has given to the Throne the power of a personal attachment. He has brought it into the hearts of his subjects. For they have discerned in their Sovereign a man whom they could understand, respect, and trust. They have seen in him a quiet dignity worthy of his high office, and with it an unaffected friendliness. They have seen a constant care for their welfare and an unselfish devotion to their service. In times of crisis— before, during, and after the War—they have found in his own calmness and steadfastness an inspiration and an example. They have rejoiced in his association with their sports and pleasures; yet they have felt that his life was founded, as they instinctively desire the life of themselves and of their country to be founded—on the faith and fear of God. Thus, in the passage of the years, he has come to be not the King only but the father of his people, and to loyalty has been added the warmth of love. This is the secret of the real personal emotion which to-day fills the heart of his Realm and Empire.

In that common heart a special place of honour and affection has been won by our gracious Queen, unwearied in her care for the health, the happiness, the homes of all the people. The Prince of Wales and the Royal Family have brought to all classes and to all parts of the world that personal touch which has moved the whole Empire to adopt the King's family as its own.

For all that our King has meant for us and has given to us, and for the way by which, during the stress of these five and twenty years, this people has been led, it behoves us to offer our thanksgiving to Almighty God. We lift up our eyes unto the hills from whence has come the help by which both he and they have been sustained, to that high region where, above the mists and clouds surrounding us, the Will of God, silent, patient, sure, is reigning. As we lift our hearts in thanksgiving so let us bow them in humble prayer, for our King and Queen that God may continue to bestow His blessing upon them, and for us all that He would pardon the sins we have committed, the mistakes we have made, the chances we have lost. Pray for this dear land, and for the Empire which has grown around it, that by God's help they may uphold before the world the cause of peace among all nations, the principles of liberty and justice, and the example of a community wherein all the citizens are the willing servants of the common weal. May we as a people, through all the fleeting shadows of time, see and follow the light which comes from that ideal and eternal city whose maker and builder is God.

When we have thus presented our vows and prayers for King and country before the Throne of our fathers' God we shall close our thanksgiving by singing the old time-honoured words, and within them to-day we shall concentrate the gratitude, the hopes, the loyalty of our hearts—

## God Save the King

# THE BROADCAST MESSAGES

## FROM HIS MAJESTY'S OVERSEAS DOMINIONS

Commencing at 7.40 p.m., MAY 6th, 1935.

### The Dominion of Canada

*Broadcast from Ottawa by*
*The Rt. Hon. Sir George H. Perley, Acting Prime Minister.*

It is my proud privilege to convey to His Majesty the King the heartfelt thanksgiving and devoted fidelity of his Canadian subjects on the celebration of the twenty-fifth anniversary of His Majesty's accession to the Throne of his fathers. During the 25 years of His Majesty's reign he has led his people through stirring times, through dark days of armed conflict and the challenging problem of peace, through the testing period of economic adversity and the return of prosperity, through the varied manifestations of a changing social order and the constitutional expressions of a developing commonwealth. Throughout, His Majesty's people in all parts of the Empire have looked to the Throne as their link with one another and with the glorious traditions of the past. We rejoice with His Majesty and with Her Majesty the Queen on this happy day, and earnestly hope that they may long be spared to strengthen the ties of affection and devotion which bind us to His Majesty's Throne and Person.

### The Commonwealth of Australia

*Broadcast from Sydney by*
*The Rt. Hon. Earle C. G. Page, Acting Prime Minister.*

I tender loyal and affectionate greetings to His Majesty the King from the people of Australia. Upon this great occasion we review with pleasure and wonder the arduous and fruitful years of his reign. We have passed through the tribulation of war to nationhood in his service, but tribulation has merely strengthened ties that bind us, and means has emphasized our unity. Conquest of the air and of the ether has given new and majestic meaning to bonds of Empire. Never was the Empire so large; never so small; for distance and time have been obliterated by the triumphant march of its people. We in Australia

14

reaffirm our loyalty to the Throne and the Person of His Majesty, and our allegiance is changed only in its deeper fervour and its added strength.

## The Dominion of New Zealand
*Broadcast from Wellington by*
*The Hon. E. A. Ransom, Acting Prime Minister.*

The Dominion of New Zealand warmly appreciates the privilege of joining in this Empire-wide broadcast in celebration of the Silver Jubilee of His Majesty King George the Fifth. New Zealand—the Britain of the South—prides itself on its British descent and on its devotion to the Crown and to the British Commonwealth of Nations. In no part of the King's Dominions is there a fuller or more heartfelt appreciation of the selfless way in which His Majesty has performed the duties of his exalted office. As the representative of every section of the people of the Dominion of New Zealand—both Pakeha and Maori—I extend our most affectionate and respectful congratulations to His Majesty and the Queen, and express our very earnest prayers that they may long be spared to continue their beneficent efforts to the good of all the British peoples.

## The Union of South Africa
*Broadcast from Cape Town by*
*Gen. The Rt. Hon. J. C. Smuts, Acting Prime Minister.*

On behalf of the Government and the people of South Africa, I beg to convey to His Majesty our sincere congratulations on his Jubilee. We are profoundly grateful that in a period which is one of the most poignant in all human history, and during which other empires of the world have disappeared, his Empire has survived grave dangers and has on the contrary received a new birth of freedom and equality in the rise of the British Commonwealth of Nations. The Union of South Africa in particular rejoice in their own Jubilee, which coincides with that of the King, and in their emergence as a united free nation in that Commonwealth. While we rejoice over our good fortune during His Majesty's reign, we specially treasure the high example of personal service and single-minded devotion to duty which His Majesty has set all his subjects during that great epoch. To him and to the Queen we respectfully give our devotion, loyalty, and affection.

## Newfoundland

*Broadcast from St. John's by*
*The Hon. F. C. Alderdice, The Official Speaker.*

In the name of the people of Newfoundland, loyal greetings and good wishes to His Majesty the King on this occasion of his Silver Jubilee. From Cape Race in the south to Cape Chidley, the northernmost point of Labrador, 300,000 Newfoundlanders join with the rest of the Empire in to-day's celebrations. Newfoundland remembers her history of over 400 years' association with the British Crown. We are the oldest Colony of Great Britain, and with that thought ever present in our minds we are proud to-day to greet His Majesty the King.

## The Indian Empire

*Broadcast from Simla by*
*His Excellency the Viceroy, The Rt. Hon. the Viscount Willingdon.*

On behalf of the Princes and people of India, I beg to send to His Majesty the King Emperor our respectful and joyful greetings on this auspicious day and to express the profound hope that he may be spared many years to continue to rule over this great country. Loyalty to the King Emperor is, and always has been, the abiding faith of the Indian people, and while it is impossible in these days of changes and development to expect the many millions of India to be free from all the stress and strain which comes with the desire for political advance, His Majesty the King Emperor can rest assured that he is held to be above and apart from such movements and that we are all devotedly loyal to the King Emperor's Throne and Person; we gratefully thank him for the constant and abiding interest he has always taken in the welfare, prosperity, and progress of all his subjects in India.

## Southern Rhodesia

*Broadcast from Salisbury by*
*The Hon. P. D. L. Fynn, Acting Prime Minister.*

Southern Rhodesia, the youngest self-governing Colony under the Crown, is proud and happy to send this first direct message of congratulation to His Majesty the King on the occasion of his Silver Jubilee. The 25 years of His Majesty's reign have been momentous years for this young country. Within that period many of our people have settled here from various parts of the Mother Country, and from other parts of the Empire. From our small beginnings 43 years ago we have grown to prosperity and responsibility under the Crown. So during His Majesty's reign Southern Rhodesia has grown to manhood. It is with special thankfulness that I send in the name of all our people, a message of loyalty and devotion to His Majesty the King.

## Bermuda

*Broadcast from Hamilton by*
*His Excellency the Governor, Lt.-Gen. Sir T. Astley Cubitt.*

It is our privilege to form the last link in the chain of greetings which the peoples of the British Empire are to-day sending to His Majesty the King. On behalf of the people of these islands I send to His Majesty the King congratulations on this celebration of the twenty-fifth year of his reign.

The people of Bermuda recall to-day that, although they form one of the smallest communities of the British Empire, they were one of the first to enjoy Representative Government. The Bermuda House of Assembly is the oldest legislative body of its kind within the Empire apart from the House of Commons.

In the name of the people of Bermuda and in the name of all the other Colonial dependencies, Bermuda sends loyal greetings to His Majesty the King and a heartfelt wish that his reign may long continue in peace and happiness.

## Northern Ireland

*The following message was received by telegram from Government House, Belfast, dispatched by His Grace the Duke of Abercorn, Governor of Northern Ireland.*

With my humble duty, I beg Your Majesties to accept from all the people of Northern Ireland our deepest respect and heartfelt congratulations on this your Silver Jubilee day, and the prayer of your people is that Your Majesties may in health and happiness be long spared to reign over them.

# THE PRIME MINISTER'S MESSAGE ON BEHALF OF THE PEOPLE OF GREAT BRITAIN

*Broadcast from London by*
THE RT. HON. J. RAMSAY MACDONALD
AT 7.58 p.m., MAY 6th, 1935

From the Dominions, from India, from Colonies and Dependencies, and all over the globe, we have been hearing greetings and expressions of loyalty and respect to His Majesty on this happy day. Now, at the close, the old original home of the British race speaks; and on its behalf I offer to the King our loyal homage and our heartfelt congratulations and thankfulness on this date.

He has reigned over us for 25 years—years of happy prosperity and of grave anxiety; long years of war, and longer years when the qualities of our people have been tested by an iron test of endurance to maintain liberty in the State, to recover from the economic destruction which is the inheritance left to our generation, to search for solutions for baffling problems in industry and in human conditions. Through these troubled years His Majesty has been reigning, wearing a heavy crown not only with regal dignity and graciousness, but with human understanding, feeling, and anxiety. His advisers have come and have gone, but for him there has been no respite. Days have mounted into months, months into years, and he has had to endure, winning, however, the devotion of all his people, and especially those who have been called to understand and to serve him.

We thank him to-night alike for his actions and for his example, and we should desire also most respectfully to pay our homage to her, whose counsel and comfort have helped and cheered him through all the years he has reigned over us—the Queen. May their years together still be many and happy. God bless them both is the fervent prayer of all their people.

Their Majesties, the King and Queen, at the Thanksgiving Service in St. Paul's Cathedral.

*Times*

HIS MAJESTY AT THE MICROPHONE

# HIS MAJESTY'S MESSAGE
# TO HIS PEOPLES

*Broadcast*
*From Buckingham Palace*

AT 8 p.m., 6th MAY, 1935

AT the close of this memorable day I must speak to my people everywhere. Yet how can I express what is in my heart? As I passed this morning through cheering multitudes to and from St. Paul's Cathedral, as I thought there of all that these twenty-five years have brought to me and to my country and my Empire, how could I fail to be most deeply moved? Words cannot express my thoughts and feelings. I can only say to you, my very dear people, that the Queen and I thank you from the depth of our hearts for all the loyalty and—may I say?—the love with which this day and always you have surrounded us. I dedicate myself anew to your service for the years that may still be given to me.

I look back on the past with thankfulness to God. My people and I have come through great trials and difficulties together. They are not over. In the midst of this day's rejoicing I grieve to think of the numbers of my people who are still without work. We owe to them, and not least to those who are suffering from any form of disablement, all the sympathy and help that we can give.

I hope that during this Jubilee Year all who can will do their utmost to find them work and bring them hope.

Other anxieties may be in store. But I am persuaded that with God's help they may all be overcome, if we meet them with confidence, courage, and unity. So I look forward to the future with faith and hope.

It is to the young that the future belongs. I trust that through the Fund inaugurated by my dear son, the Prince of Wales, to commemorate this year, many of them throughout this country may be helped in body, mind, and character to become useful citizens.

To the children I would like to send a special message. Let me say this to each of them whom my words may reach:—The King is speaking to *you*. I ask you to remember that in days to come you will be the citizens of a great Empire. As you grow up always keep this thought before you; and when the time comes be ready and proud to give to your country the service of your work, your mind, and your heart.

I have been greatly touched by all the greetings which have come to me to-day from my Dominions and Colonies, from India, and from this home country. My heart goes out to all who may be listening to me now wherever you may be—here at home in town or village, or in some far-off corner of the Empire, or it may be on the high seas.

Let me end my words to you with those which Queen Victoria used after her Diamond Jubilee, 38 years ago. No words could more truly or simply express my own deep feeling now: "From my heart I thank my beloved people. May God bless them."

# HIS
# MAJESTY'S
# RECEPTION

## OF REPRESENTATIVES OF THE CORPS DIPLOMATIQUE AND OF HIS MAJESTY'S OVERSEAS DOMINIONS

## *At St. James's Palace*

### MAY 8TH, 1935

ON Wednesday, May the Eighth, 1935, His Majesty the King and Her Majesty the Queen drove to St. James's Palace and held a reception of the Representatives of the Corps Diplomatique and of His Majesty's Overseas Dominions.

Their Royal Highnesses the Prince of Wales, the Duke of York, the Duke of Gloucester and the Duke of Kent were present.

His Excellency the Brazilian Ambassador, Senhor Paul Regis de Oliveira, as the doyen of the Corps Diplomatique, addressed congratulations to the King and Queen on behalf of the Heads of Missions accredited to the Court of St. James's, to which His Majesty replied.

## THE BRAZILIAN AMBASSADOR'S ADDRESS ON BEHALF OF THE CORPS DIPLOMATIQUE

YOUR MAJESTY:—

I am more deeply moved than I can say by the honour of being called upon to express to Your Majesty, in the name of the Heads of Missions accredited to the Court of St. James's, our most respectful feelings and our warmest wishes on this occasion when Your Majesty and Her Majesty the Queen, surrounded by the deep devotion of all the peoples of the Empire, are celebrating their Silver Jubilee.

The representatives of foreign countries desire to associate themselves with equal joy and sincerity in those demonstrations which have conveyed to Your Majesty from the United Kingdom, the whole Empire, and every part of the world, the heartfelt expression of the affectionate respect for the august Sovereign whose courage, wisdom, and goodness are the admiration of the world, whilst his personal authority has invariably been exercised for the creation of that spirit of good understanding and co-operation which may be counted as one of the fundamental bases of peace.

Your Majesty's reign, filled with glory and achievement, stands in the record of our age as among the worthiest in the history of this great and friendly Empire, which is itself one of the foundations of our common civilization.

The honour which falls to me of representing Brazil, whose relations of time-honoured friendship with the United Kingdom date from the moment of our Independence, and have remained unchanged through all the days of our Empire and our Republic, is multiplied to-day by the rare happiness of speaking in the name of the Heads of Missions.

Since the day of Your Majesty's Accession new nations have swelled the number of Foreign Missions accredited to this ancient and historic Court, and it thus comes about that the Corps Diplomatique has the honour to gather round Your Majesty's august Person to-day, at once the largest and the fullest representation of the thought and feeling of the entire world.

Deeply conscious of the honour of our Mission to Your Majesty, we would ask for a continuance of that Royal kindliness which we feel to be our greatest encouragement in the discharge of our duties.

The Heads of Missions accredited to the Court of St. James's therefore beg Your Majesty to be good enough graciously to accept this expression of their devotion, of their heartfelt and respectful congratulations on this twenty-fifth anniversary of Your Majesty's Accession and of their trust that Divine Providence may grant to Your Majesty, Her Majesty the Queen, the Prince of Wales, and the Royal Family long years of happiness and prosperity.

# HIS MAJESTY'S REPLY

TO HIS EXCELLENCY THE BRAZILIAN AMBASSADOR

YOUR EXCELLENCY:—The warmth and sincerity of the congratulations and good wishes which you have just addressed to me in the name of the Diplomatic Body accredited to my Court, have deeply touched the Queen and myself. It is particularly gratifying to me that these words should have been pronounced by one whose long residence in London and whose well-known friendship for my country have won for him an especial esteem, not only as an individual but as the representative of a great and friendly Republic with which our relations are, and have always been, peculiarly happy.

Your Excellency has rightly called attention to the gradual increase in the number of States represented at my Court; it is a pleasure to me, and, I hope a happy augury for the future, that envoys from every quarter of the globe are assembled here to-day in amity and goodwill.

I have heard it rumoured that amongst your colleagues my capital is a greatly coveted post. I am indeed happy if that is the case, and, just as I consider my Court to be singularly well favoured in respect of the representatives accredited to it, so it will be my unfailing endeavour to ensure that no support or encouragement of which they may stand in need shall ever be lacking.

Your Excellency, once more I thank you and your colleagues, on my own behalf and in the name of the Queen and of my Family, for your kind expressions of goodwill. I deeply appreciate and heartily reciprocate them; and I pray God that the unity of purpose which has brought you here together to-day may be a symbol of an enduring peace in the world at large.

AFTER HIS MAJESTY'S REPLY TO HIS EXCELLENCY THE BRAZILIAN AMBASSADOR, THE FOLLOWING PRESENTED ADDRESSES TO HIS MAJESTY ON BEHALF OF HIS OVERSEAS DOMINIONS:—

THE RIGHT HON. R. B. BENNETT,
*Prime Minister of the Dominion of Canada.*

THE RIGHT HON. J. A. LYONS,
*Prime Minister of the Commonwealth of Australia.*

THE RIGHT HON. G. W. FORBES,
*Prime Minister of the Dominion of New Zealand.*

GENERAL THE HON. J. B. M. HERTZOG,
*Prime Minister of the Union of South Africa.*

THE RIGHT HON. J. H. THOMAS,
*Secretary of State for Dominion Affairs.*

SIR JOSEPH BHORE,
*Representative of the Indian Government.*

THE HON. G. M. HUGGINS,
*Prime Minister of Southern Rhodesia.*

THE RIGHT HON. SIR PHILIP CUNLIFFE-LISTER,
*Secretary of State for the Colonies.*

THE RIGHT HON. SIR JOHN GILMOUR, BT.,
*Secretary of State for Home Affairs.*

*The text of these Addresses is given in the following pages.*

# THE ADDRESSES FROM HIS MAJESTY'S OVERSEAS DOMINIONS

### MAY 8th, 1935

## THE RIGHT HON. R. B. BENNETT,
*Prime Minister of the Dominion of Canada.*

YOUR MAJESTY:—I have the high privilege and great honour humbly to offer to Your Majesty, on behalf of the people and the Government of Canada, a message of loyal devotion and respectful congratulations. We render praise and thanksgiving to the Almighty that our King, whose counsels have ever been directed to the glory of God and the welfare of his people, has been spared to reach the twenty-fifth year of his reign.

During this period, events have occurred of a magnitude and consequence never before recorded in the history of the world. The clash of armed strife has been followed by the turmoil of economic and political adjustment. There has been no calm after storm; no peace after conflict. It has been a time that tested as never before the qualities alike of nations and of individuals. That the British Empire has successfully withstood this test has been due in no small measure to the fact that you, Sir, have given us the inspiration of wise and tactful leadership, unselfish patriotism, and unswerving devotion to duty.

Under your Sovereignty, the Empire has witnessed far-reaching changes through constitutional evolution. These changes, however, have served but to strengthen our loyalty to the Throne and to deepen our sentiments of affection and devotion towards Your Majesty. To-day, Sir, through you, the people of your vast Empire are united in one Family of Nations.

May I add, Sir, that your gracious consort, Her Majesty the Queen, shares in our hearts the place held by Your Majesty. We remember, at this time, your words on ascending the Throne: 'I am encouraged by the knowledge that I have in my dear wife one who will be a constant helpmate in every endeavour for our peoples' good.' No Queen has associated herself more sympathetically or effectively with a reigning Sovereign in supporting the Throne. I hope, Sir, it is not unfitting for me to state that our King and Queen, in their life and work together, have given the peoples of the Empire an example which has strengthened and ennobled that conception of family life which is the true basis of all human happiness and national greatness.

I speak for every citizen of Your Majesty's Dominion of Canada, wherever he may dwell, when I pledge anew our allegiance, and vouchsafe the earnest hope that Your Majesty may long continue under Providence to lead your people along the paths of peace, prosperity, and honour.


## THE RIGHT HON. J. A. LYONS,
*Prime Minister of the Commonwealth of Australia.*

YOUR MAJESTY:—I consider it a signal honour to be the instrument through which are conveyed to you the loyal greetings of the people of the Commonwealth of Australia.

It is also my privilege to bring their congratulations that you and the Queen are celebrating the Silver Jubilee of your illustrious reign, and their fervent wish that for many more years you will be spared to rule over the great Empire to which they are so proud to belong.

Australia lies far distant from the shores of Britain, but our loyalty to the Throne and Person of Your Majesty is not lessened by the thousands of miles of land and sea which separate us from you; rather has it been strengthened by them, deepened by the knowledge that across half the globe there dwells a Monarch who understands and

The Presentation of the Pearl Sword to His Majesty by the Lord Mayor of London.

Their Majesties passing through Fleet Street in The Silver Jubilee Procession.

sympathizes with our problems as much as he understands and sympathizes with those of his subjects in the Homeland.

You have honoured us from time to time by sending to visit us members of your family, and we remember with affection that you yourself are no stranger to our shores. Your sons will have told you of the loyalty of the people of Australia to the Empire, and I assure Your Majesty that the loyalty of the Australian people was never stronger than it is now, and that, as far as Australia is concerned, never was there greater devotion and respect to the head of the Empire.

May I quote a verse written recently by an Australian, William Tainsh?—

> Our Sovereign Lord, the years of your high labours
> Have held scant measuring of sunlit days;
> So, for your splendid bearing in the shadows,
> Yours be the greater love, the greater praise.

Your life has been an inspiration to all your subjects; for the dignity, courage, wisdom, and self-sacrifice which you have shown during the twenty-five years of your arduous reign have been an example worthy of being followed by every Briton.

Humbly and sincerely, I tender to Your Majesty this message of loyalty from one of your most distant Dominions. It is a message of love, as much as of loyalty, and a message of pride that we are able to share in the glory of your reign.

## THE RIGHT HON. G. W. FORBES,
*Prime Minister of the Dominion of New Zealand.*

YOUR MAJESTY:—I come from New Zealand charged with the duty, which it is my pleasure and honour to fulfil, of conveying to Your Majesty the most hearty congratulations of the people of that Dominion, both Pakeha and Maori, on the occasion of the Silver Jubilee of Your Majesty's beneficent reign.

We take the greatest pleasure in associating ourselves with the celebrations which are being held throughout the British Commonwealth to mark the event, and are entering wholeheartedly into the spirit of rejoicing which assuredly prevails among the citizens of the Empire.

You have led your peoples through an epoch of unprecedented difficulties and achievements, and the unity of our Empire and the prominent position it holds in the world to-day are mainly due to the leadership and inspiration which have characterized your reign.

Your subjects in New Zealand preserve indelible memories of the noble courage and self-sacrifice Your Majesties and other members of the Royal Family showed during the dark days of the War, and, later, through the hardships of the world-wide economic depression, your unfailing sympathy with all sections of your sorely-tried people has been a source of comfort and encouragement.

Although we are the furthermost Dominion of the Empire, the progress and improvement in transportation and communication are ever bringing us closer to the Motherland, the home of our kith and kin, but the people of the Britain of the South do not require the aid of science or invention to strengthen their loyalty and affection to Your Majesty. Our earnest desire is to be worthy in every respect of the race from which we have sprung.

The citizens of New Zealand have the happiest recollections of Your Majesties' sojourn among us in 1901, and deeply appreciate Your Majesty's gracious action in permitting your sons to visit us in more recent years. We look upon these visits as precious links with the British Crown.

It is our fervent prayer that you may long be spared to guide the destinies of our Empire, and that Her Majesty the Queen may continue her companionship with you through many years of peace and happiness.

## GENERAL THE HON. J. B. M. HERTZOG,
### Prime Minister of the Union of South Africa.

YOUR MAJESTY:—Amidst the many cordial proofs of joyous homage on this happy occasion, may it please Your Majesty also to accept the very hearty congratulations of the people and the Government of your Union of South Africa, together with the sincere assurance of our loyalty to you, Sire, as our Sovereign, a loyalty which, with very many, and more especially with those of British descent, has evoked deep sentiments of love and devotion to Your Majesty's person.

With the great majority not so descended, the remembrance that it was during Your Majesty's reign that the Union attained its proud status as an independent Sovereign State and equal partner in the British Commonwealth of Nations, will ever fill them with feelings of deep gratitude and with the sincere desire and determination to be faithfully obedient to the laws of the Union, and Your Majesty's commands as their Sovereign.

The happy memories associated with the attainment of that status will ever serve as so many links in the close and friendly co-operation between the Union and the rest of the British Commonwealth of Nations, over whose happiness and prosperity may Your Majesty be spared to preside for many years to come.


## THE RIGHT HON. J. H. THOMAS,
### *Secretary of State for Dominion Affairs.*

YOUR MAJESTY:—I am charged to-day to convey to Your Majesty and to Her Majesty the Queen the loyal and affectionate greetings of the people of Newfoundland.

The oldest Colony yields place to none in its deep-rooted devotion to Your Majesty's Person and Throne, and in none of Your Majesty's Possessions is there more sincere rejoicing on this happy occasion of the twenty-fifth anniversary of Your Majesty's Accession.

Newfoundland has played a notable part in the development of the British Commonwealth, culminating in the splendid achievements of her sons in the Great War. In the economic vicissitudes that have overtaken the world in recent years the Island has suffered more perhaps than any part of the Empire, but the steadfast courage and endurance of her people are a guarantee that she will once more triumph over her difficulties.

The people of Newfoundland unite in thankfulness to Almighty God that Your Majesty has been spared to preside over the destinies of the British Family of Nations in this period of momentous change, and they pray that Your

Majesty, Her Gracious Majesty the Queen, and Your Royal House, firmly established in the affection of your people, may be blessed with happiness and prosperity in the years to come.

It is also my privilege to convey to Your Majesty the loyal and heartfelt congratulations of the people of Basutoland, the Bechuanaland Protectorate, and Swaziland.

## SIR JOSEPH BHORE,
*Representative of the Indian Government.*

YOUR MAJESTY:—India joins with the rest of the Empire in offering to Your Majesty respectful congratulations on this auspicious occasion. The past 25 years have been a period of notable advance in the history of India, and it is with gratitude that we recall Your Majesty's constant interest in, and deep solicitude for, the people of India, their progress and well-being. Nor can we forget the gracious sympathy which Her Majesty the Queen has ever extended to all efforts for the furtherance of the welfare of India's women and children.

Devotion to the Sovereign and loyalty to the Throne have been the traditional characteristics of the Indian people since the governance of India passed to the British Crown, and those traditions are as strong to-day as they were when Queen Victoria won for herself and her Imperial line the deep and abiding affection of the Indian people.

India to-day stands on the threshold of great changes. It is our earnest prayer that those changes may bring lasting peace and contentment to Your Majesty's Indian subjects, and that Your Majesty's reign, already so rich in beneficent results, may be rendered unique in the annals of Indian history. The people of India offer Your Majesty and Her Majesty the Queen their loyal and respectful homage. Throughout the vast Indian Empire Your Majesty's loyal subjects will in temple, in mosque, in church, in places of worship belonging to every creed and faith, be offering prayers that Your Majesties may long be spared to them and to the Empire.

34

## THE HON. G. M. HUGGINS,
### *Prime Minister of Southern Rhodesia.*

YOUR MAJESTY:—Your Majesty's gracious command has made it possible for me to convey in person to Your Majesty the congratulations, gratitude, humble loyalty and love of your subjects in Southern Rhodesia.

The Europeans, Natives, and Asiatics, in this, the youngest of Your Majesty's self-governing States, are one in their pride of membership of the Great Realm which owes allegiance to Your Majesty. They are also one in their determination to live worthy of Your Majesty's pleasure, and in their eagerness to co-operate with their fellow subjects throughout the world in maintaining the security and prosperity of Your Majesty's Empire.

When Your Majesty granted the functions of responsible government to Southern Rhodesia, a great responsibility was placed upon those of European descent on account of the very large number of primitive African people committed to their care.

We hope and believe that, with Divine guidance, and following the noble example set before us by Your Majesty, and the principles traditional to our race, of justice and humanity, and with an earnest desire to help and raise those less fortunate than ourselves, we shall prove worthy of that trust.

The people of Southern Rhodesia one and all pray that Your Majesty and Her Majesty the Queen may long be spared to continue to guide the destinies and influence the hearts and minds of your loyal and loving subjects.


## THE RIGHT HON. SIR PHILIP CUNLIFFE-LISTER,
### *Secretary of State for the Colonies.*

YOUR MAJESTY:—On behalf of all Your Majesty's subjects in the many lands of your Colonial Empire, I offer you, Sir, their loyal and heartfelt congratulations.

Many of these countries are well known to Your Majesty personally, and the proud memory of your own visits, Sir, has been renewed by those of Members of your

Family, whom they have rejoiced to honour. Throughout these distant lands, your Jubilee has been celebrated, and Your Majesty's own message has been heard.

Infinite in their variety of race and creed and rule, the peoples of these lands are one in personal devotion to Your Majesty and in loyalty to your Throne. Everywhere they are mindful of the wise and gracious solicitude with which you have ever watched over their interests and promoted their welfare, a solicitude in which Her Majesty the Queen has conspicuously shared. It is their earnest prayer that Your Majesty may long be spared to continue your high Imperial task.

## THE RIGHT HON. SIR JOHN GILMOUR, BT.,
### *Secretary of State for Home Affairs.*

YOUR MAJESTY:—It is my privilege to-day to speak on behalf of certain parts of Your Majesty's dominions which are not often referred to but are those most intimately connected with Great Britain. I refer to Northern Ireland, which is part of the United Kingdom, and to the islands of Jersey and Guernsey and its Dependencies, which are a surviving part of the ancient Duchy of Normandy. There is also the Isle of Man, which was formerly ruled by the Lords of Man and is now attached to your Kingdom.

All these are conspicuous for their affection towards Your Majesty and their loyalty to your Throne. On behalf of their Legislatures and peoples I have the honour to express their affectionate regard for Your Majesty and for Her Majesty the Queen and to offer to Your Majesty their loyal congratulations on your having completed 25 years of your reign, with their heartfelt wishes that you may long be spared to rule over them.

# HIS MAJESTY'S REPLY
## TO THE REPRESENTATIVES
## OF THE OVERSEAS DOMINIONS
### MAY 8th, 1935

THERE is a word which gladdens me, more especially when I hear it used by friends from overseas, many of whom say when they visit this country that "they are coming home." It is in this spirit that the Queen and I meet you to-day, you who represent the vast territories of the Dominions, Colonies, and the Protectorates, my peoples of India, and the dwellers in countless isles of the sea, from the Pacific to our own home waters. We greet the Prime Ministers of the Dominions, now equal partners in the Empire, and I thank them for the Addresses from their Parliaments which they have handed to me. We welcome one and all to our home.

Eventful your visit cannot fail to be: I trust that it will be happy also. And, when the time comes for you to return, I would ask you to take back each to his own people, a message of affection to every member of this great family of which I am so proud and thankful to be the Head: and a message of deep gratitude for the loyal and kind words which you have spoken on their behalf. You all who are here to-day, and who hold responsible positions, will best know what an inspiration and encouragement your words are to me to continue the task which 25 years ago I set myself to do.

Before I succeeded my father, the Queen and I had the privilege of studying at first hand the Dominions Overseas and India. We were fellow travellers, then as now, comparing notes and sharing impressions. We treasure these memories and keep them alive; moreover, what we forget our four sons are now able to recall. Many years before our happy partnership began I had as a midshipman sailed the seven seas : I realized early that the Empire has many climes but one spirit.

I regard this as a unique gathering, where we can tell one another of our successes, and also of our failures and mistakes. But there will be no sharp criticism nor vain regrets, for we are in sympathy, one with another, conscious that we have acted according to our lights, for the good name and ordered prosperity of the family.

We are sometimes told that we are lacking in logic, our political institutions loose and undefined. But I look back on the trying and testing time through which we have passed and wonder whether a less flexible system would have withstood the strains to which we have been subjected. With commonsense and goodwill as our shield and buckler, we have kept, in spite of all difficulties, our heritage of liberty, alike for the individual and for our many constituent races. The numberless and invisible ties of sentiment and tradition which bind us together are indeed delicate; but many strands make a cable, strong to bind in times of adversity. It is my prayer, no less than my firm belief, that this bond of the spirit may prove also the bond of peace.

Some of you are, with a few happy exceptions, about my own age. I pray for the continuance of God's blessing on your labours. With His help I will work on with you in the years that remain for that object which has ever been next my heart—the welfare of the Mother Country, of the Dominions Overseas, and of India, their happiness and their good repute.

The Procession in Trafalgar Square on the way to St. Paul's Cathedral.

The Presentation of the Addresses by the Lords and Commons to His Majesty in Westminster Hall.

# THE PRESENTATION
# OF ADDRESSES

## TO HIS MAJESTY
## BY HIS LORDS
## AND COMMONS

### At the Palace of Westminster
### MAY 9TH, 1935

ON Thursday, May the Ninth, 1935, His Majesty the King and Her Majesty the Queen drove to the Palace of Westminster and, in the historic Westminster Hall received Addresses from the House of Lords and the House of Commons, to which His Majesty replied.

Their Royal Highnesses the Prince of Wales, the Duke and Duchess of York, the Duke of Gloucester and the Duke and Duchess of Kent, the Princess Royal and the Earl of Harewood, and Princess Alice and the Earl of Athlone were present.

The Address from the House of Lords was read and presented to His Majesty by The Lord Chancellor and the Address from the House of Commons by The Speaker.

## THE ADDRESS FROM THE HOUSE OF LORDS

MOST GRACIOUS MAJESTY:—

WE, Your Majesty's dutiful and loyal subjects, the Lords Spiritual and Temporal in Parliament assembled, beg leave to offer to Your Majesty our most heartfelt congratulations on the completion of the twenty-fifth year of your reign. With every one of Your Majesty's subjects, whether within the United Kingdom or in the most distant corners of Your Majesty's Dominions, we give thanks to Almighty God for the blessing and protection bestowed upon Your Majesty during these five and twenty years; and we pray that for many years to come Your Majesty may continue to rule over us in health and strength and happiness.

This City of Westminster, this Hall wherein we meet, tell the story of the growth through centuries of civil liberty and the rule of law, of that ordered freedom which is the pride and heritage of our race. In comparison with these long centuries, twenty-five years may seem but a short span of time. They have been years of struggle and anxiety as well as of resolute achievement. Into them have been crowded the fierce ordeal of the most desolating War in history, the toil of rebuilding the shaken structure of our common life, the slow and arduous endeavour to regain prosperity and to establish peace. Elsewhere Thrones and Constitutions have failed to outlast the strain. Yet in this Realm the development of public rights and liberties has not been arrested but has been made wider and more sure. More truly than any of your illustrious ancestors, Your Majesty rules over a Nation of free citizens. Yet in spite of, nay, rather because of, this wide extension of government by the people, the Throne stands more firmly than ever before as the centre of the national life.

Beyond the seas there have been other, perhaps even greater, changes. During Your Majesty's reign free institutions have sprung into being and have flourished throughout your Empire, and in your Parliament of Westminster Your Majesty has marked the growth of your self-governing Dominions by the declaration of their authentic place in that association which we know as the British Commonwealth of Nations.

Your Majesty's own personality has made the Throne not merely a symbol, but a loved and living reality. For in the Sovereign your subjects have discerned a man who, by simply being himself, has commanded their respect and appealed to their hearts. In time of war the standard-bearer of the national spirit, in the anxious years which followed a counsellor wise and steadfast, seeking not your own but ever mindful of the needs and cares of all your people, avoiding no hardship and shrinking from no sacrifice, Your Majesty has called forth a loyalty and love which have given a new meaning to the name of King.

We venture also to offer our loyal homage and respectful congratulations to Our Gracious Queen, who has shared with Your Majesty the toils and triumphs of these five and twenty years. By her unfailing interest in the lives and homes of the people, Her Majesty has won a place of her own in their affection. When we see gathered round Your Majesties your sons, always and in every part of the world active in the public service, we have a sure confidence that, when this generation has passed and the bright pageantry of this week has become a distant memory, the House of Windsor will still reign over a loyal and united people.

In no formal manner, but from the depth of our hearts, we pray—God bless Your Majesty.


## THE ADDRESS FROM THE HOUSE OF COMMONS

WE, Your Majesty's faithful Commons, desire to offer our humble congratulations on the completion of twenty-five years of your Reign, our assurance of our loyal devotion to your Person and your House, and our heartfelt gratitude for what you have done for your country and your people.

On Your Majesty's Accession to the Throne we ventured to use these words—that we were convinced "that your reign, under the favour of Divine Providence, would be distinguished by unswerving efforts to promote the virtue, prosperity and contentment of the realm and to guard the rights and liberties of Your Majesty's faithful people." That hope has been abundantly fulfilled.

Our Constitution has proved itself strong enough to withstand the shock of a great war, and flexible enough to adapt itself to the changing circumstances of the Empire and the world. It has given the nation stability when elsewhere foundations were crumbling. While retaining its historic features, it has been broadened to give expression to the will of the whole people on an extended franchise, and under it Your Majesty's Governments have been able, without breach of continuity, to undertake new responsibilities on behalf of the public weal.

Your Majesty's reign has seen profound changes in world conditions, and the consequent emergence of complex and unfamiliar problems. We may humbly claim that our historic forms of government have proved themselves adequate to meet each crisis as it arose. Our traditional policy has varied its methods in order to preserve its essentials. Britain remains, as ever, a free and a well-ordered nation.

These years record a continuous process of development in the Empire of which Your Majesty is Sovereign. The Colonies have grown in economic and political stature. We have now before us constitutional proposals designed widely to extend the measure of self-Government inaugurated in India fourteen years ago. Statutory recognition has been given by Parliament to the new structure of our partnership with the Dominions as free, equal, and autonomous States united by a common allegiance to the Crown.

Your Majesty's high office has been enriched by the personality of him who holds it. You have shared in the nation's trials and triumphs; You have sorrowed and rejoiced with your people; Your wisdom and fortitude have steadied the national temper; with the gracious aid of the Queen, you have won by your sympathy and kindliness something warmer than allegiance and profounder than loyalty. To-day you are more than Sovereign; You are Head of the Family, and of a Nation and an Empire you have made a Household.

Twenty-five years ago you defined the tasks of a Sovereign as "the safeguarding of the treasures of the past" and "the preparing of the path of the future." Your Majesty has nobly fulfilled both duties. We look back with grateful hearts upon the past, and with confidence we await the future. We offer you, with deep respect and affection, the homage of a free Parliament, and we pray that, by the blessing of Almighty God, you will long continue to be the Sovereign of a proud and devoted People.

Mayors of London Boroughs being presented during one of Their Majesties' Drives through London.

Their Majesties on the Balcony at Buckingham Palace after their return from the Thanksgiving Service.  Left to right: H.M. The Queen of Norway, H.R.H. The Duke of York, H.R.H. The Princess Royal, H.M. The King, H.R.H. Princess Margaret of York, The Hon. Gerald Lascelles,

The Earl of Harewood, H.R.H. Princess Elizabeth of York, Viscount Lascelles, H.M. the Queen, H.R.H. The Duke of Gloucester, H.R.H. The Duchess of Kent, H.R.H. The Duke of Kent, H.R.H. The Duchess of York, H.R.H. Princess Victoria, and H.R.H. The Prince of Wales.

Commemorating the Silver Jubilee: The large illustration shows the Silver Jubilee Commemorative Medal issued for the public. Below it are shown: The King's Silver Jubilee Medal with ribbon, the Jubilee stamp issued in various denominations, the reverse of the Commemorative Medal, the reverse of the King's Silver Jubilee Medal, and, at the bottom, the special crown piece.

# HIS
# MAJESTY'S
# REPLY

## TO THE ADDRESSES FROM
## HIS LORDS AND COMMONS

MAY 9TH, 1935

MY LORDS AND MEMBERS OF THE HOUSE OF COMMONS:—I thank you from my heart for your loyal Addresses, and for the words of devoted affection which you have used in speaking of myself, of the Queen, and of our Family.

Your presence here to-day, accompanied by the Prime Ministers of the Dominion of Canada, the Commonwealth of Australia, the Dominion of New Zealand and the Union of South Africa, gives rise to many memories and many thoughts. The Mother of Parliaments and her children, grown to full estate, stand now upon equal terms in common allegiance to the Crown. The unity of the British Empire is no longer expressed by the supremacy of the time-honoured Parliament that sits here at Westminster. The Crown is the historic symbol that unites this great family of nations and races, scattered over every quarter of the earth. The United Kingdom and the Dominions, India, the numerous Colonies and Dependencies, embrace such wide varieties of speech, culture and form of government as have never before in the world's history been brought into a Commonwealth of Peace. In these days, when fear and preparation for war are again astir in the world, let us be thankful that quiet government and peace prevail over so large a part of the earth's surface, and that under our flag of freedom so many millions eat their daily bread, in far distant lands and climates, with none to make them afraid.

I especially welcome here to-day representatives of my Indian Empire.

This, my Palace of Westminster, in the mighty heart of our Empire, is the very cradle of our envied Parliamentary institutions. Here is the anvil whereon our common law was forged, to become the joint inheritance of the United States of America and our own community of peoples. Beneath these rafters of mediæval oak, the silent witnesses of historic tragedies and pageants, we celebrate the present under the spell of the past.

It is to me a source of pride and thankfulness that the perfect harmony of our Parliamentary system with our Constitutional Monarchy has survived the shocks that have in recent years destroyed other Empires and other liberties. Our ancient Constitution, ever adaptable to change, has, during my reign faced and conquered perils of warfare never conceived in earlier days, and has met and satisfied new democratic demands both at home and overseas. The system bequeathed to us by our ancestors, again modified for the needs of a new age, has been found once more, as of old, the best way to secure government by the people, freedom for the individual, the ordered strength of the State and the rule of law over governors and governed alike.

The complex forms and balanced spirit of our Constitution were not the discovery of a single era, still less of a single party or of a single person. They are the slow accretion of centuries, the outcome of patience, tradition, and experience, constantly finding channels old and new for the impulse towards liberty, justice and social improvement inherent in our people down the ages.

When my Grandmother, Queen Victoria, of illustrious memory, rejoiced with her people on the occasion of her two Jubilees, she gave thanks for a long period of unbroken prosperity. Such periods cannot always recur. In looking back over the 25 years of my reign, the thankfulness that I feel to-day is chiefly for escape from danger greater than ever before threatened our land. I can never forget how the peril from without at once united all the parties, classes, Governments, and races of the Empire; men and women played their parts; the ranks were closed, and, in the issue, strength upheld the free. Let us not in this hour of thanksgiving fail to remember those who gave their lives, or who live now maimed or blinded, that we might continue to enjoy the blessings of life.

Through later years our path has led uphill. In the aftermath of war, in a world exhausted by its ordeals and impoverished by its destruction, we set ourselves to resume our normal ways, to recreate the structure of our industry and commerce, and to respond to the urgent desire to improve the conditions of life. We were treading unfamiliar and broken ground, for there had been far-reaching changes, especially in economic conditions. Everywhere a feeling of uncertainty and lack of confidence hung like a shadow over human endeavour. But we have made headway by the earnest goodwill, prudence, and stability of my people, and to-day the country has attained to a measure of industrial success which gives it confidence in the future.

I am very conscious that these years have brought hardship and often disappointment, and I have been moved with profound admiration for the great-heartedness of my people, and for the steadfast fortitude and unbending will to overcome, which they have ever shown in their anxieties. I sympathize deeply with those who have endured the sadness and burden of unemployment. It is a source of comfort to me to feel that from these times of trial there has grown up throughout our community a stronger feeling of fellowship one with another.

I have been blessed in all my work in having beside me my dear Wife, of whom you have spoken so kindly. I give thanks to Almighty God, Who has thus far sustained me and my people, and I pray that we may continue to pursue the cause of freedom and progress in a spirit of peace, tolerance, and understanding.

# HIS MAJESTY'S MESSAGE TO THE CHILDREN OF LONDON

TO the Children of London, on the twenty-fifth anniversary of my Accession, I send you this message:—

You are the heirs of a great past; but the future is yours, and is your high responsibility. Each of you must try to be a good citizen in a good city. To this end, you must make the best of all your powers.

Strive to grow in strength, in knowledge, and in grace. If you persist bravely in this endeavour you will work worthily for your family, your city, your country, and for mankind.

So to live, in whatever sphere, must be noble and may be great.

My confident trust is in you.

GEORGE R.I.

# THE JUBILEE CELEBRATIONS

*Below is a calendar of the principal Royal engagements in 1935 arranged during The Silver Jubilee Celebrations.*

| | |
|---|---|
| *Monday, May 6th:* | The Silver Jubilee Procession and Thanksgiving Service in St. Paul's Cathedral. |
| | Broadcast from Buckingham Palace of His Majesty's Message to His Peoples. |
| *Wednesday, May 8th:* | Reception at St. James's Palace of representatives of the Corps Diplomatique and of His Majesty's Overseas Dominions. |
| *Thursday, May 9th:* | Presentation of Addresses by Lords and Commons at Westminster Hall. |
| | State Dinner at Buckingham Palace. |
| *Saturday, May 11th:* | Royal Drive through North London. |
| | H.R.H. The Prince of Wales' visit to Cardiff. |
| | H.R.H. The Duke of York's visit to Edinburgh. |
| | H.R.H. The Duke of Gloucester's visit to Belfast. |
| *Tuesday, May 14th:* | Ball at Buckingham Palace. |
| *Saturday, May 18th:* | Royal Drive through South London. |
| *Monday, May 20th:* | State Dinner at Buckingham Palace. |
| *Wednesday, May 22nd:* | Reception and Ball given by The Lord Mayor and Corporation of London at Guildhall. |
| *Friday, May 24th:* | Royal Command Concert of British Music at the Royal Albert Hall. |
| *Saturday, May 25th:* | Royal Drive through East London. |
| *Friday, May 31st:* | Levée at St. James's Palace. |
| | Reception given by the London County Council at the County Hall. |
| *Monday, June 3rd:* | His Majesty's Birthday. |
| | Trooping of the Colour, Horse Guards Parade. |
| *Saturday, June 8th:* | Royal Drive through West London. |
| *Thursday, June 13th:* | Ball at Buckingham Palace. |
| *Saturday, June 15th:* | Royal Drive through Eton and Windsor. |
| *Monday, June 17th:* | Knights of the Garter Ceremony at St. George's Chapel, Windsor. |
| *Tuesday, June 25th:* | Their Majesties' Court, Buckingham Palace. |
| *Wednesday, June 26th:* | Their Majesties' Court, Buckingham Palace. |
| *Saturday, July 6th:* | His Majesty's Review of the Air Force at Mildenhall and Duxford. |
| *Tuesday, July 9th:* | Royal Investiture at Buckingham Palace. |
| *Wednesday, July 10th:* | Royal Investiture at Buckingham Palace. |
| *Saturday, July 13th:* | His Majesty's Review of the Army at Aldershot. |
| *Tuesday, July 16th:* | His Majesty's Review of the Fleet at Spithead. |
| *Saturday, July 20th:* | His Majesty's Inspection of the Police in Hyde Park, London. |
| *Thursday, July 25th:* | Their Majesties' Garden Party at Buckingham Palace. |

# KING GEORGE'S
# JUBILEE TRUST

ON March 1st, 1935, several weeks prior to the Silver Jubilee ceremonies, H.R.H. the Prince of Wales, at a meeting at St. James's Palace to which Lords-Lieutenant, Lord-Mayors, Lord Provosts, Mayors and Provosts from all over the country were invited, unfolded proposals for a national thank-offering in celebration of the twenty-five years of His Majesty's reign.

Thus was inaugurated "King George's Jubilee Trust," having as its purpose the welfare, inspiration and guidance of young people, both boys and girls, in the difficult years between the time they leave school and their attainment of maturity.

The wholehearted response which welcomed this plan is immediate proof, not only of the Nation's desire to show its thankfulness to the King and Queen, but of its unanimous approval of the purpose for which the Trust has been founded.

It is a cause that must appeal to everyone who has the future of the country at heart. Our destiny is in the hands of the rising generation. There can be no more vital task than the work of helping the young people who are entering the world under present-day difficult conditions, to become healthy and responsible citizens.

There are in Great Britain to-day over a million boys and girls between the ages of fourteen and eighteen who, through no fault of their own, are denied those opportunities of self-development to which they are entitled.

Already there are organisations doing magnificent work to provide these young people with healthy recreation, with worth-while hobbies, and with practical vocational training, instilling in their minds a moral and cultural standard that will influence them throughout their lives. It is not the purpose of the Trust to start any new movement; it will help and extend the work of those which already have so well justified their existence, often in the face of tremendous handicaps.

Clubs, gymnasia, playing fields, libraries, workshops—all are required in order adequately to meet the physical, moral and mental needs of the rising generation. In all parts of the country the need is urgent, particularly in those distressed areas where lack of funds is most pronounced. For want of adequate premises and equipment the health and happiness of hundreds of thousands of boys and girls is endangered, not only to-day but for the years ahead.

Only those whose work lies amongst young people know the gravity of this national problem. Experience proves beyond all question that juvenile crime increases in direct proportion to the lack of cultural facilities of the kind that it is the purpose of the Trust to provide.

"The street-corner boy must go." That, in a phrase, sums up the Trust's objective. The slackness, lack of purpose and low standard of living of which he is the symbol is a menace to the nation's future no less than to the boys and girls themselves, who are condemned to spend their youth without help or guidance in the healthy training of mind and body.

Success for the work of King George's Jubilee Trust will mean that the boys and girls of Britain will grow up worthy of the great heritage which is theirs. It is a great task, but it is one that can and must be accomplished.

Already splendid progress has been made, but the full development of this work demands the co-operation of all. The administration of the Trust is in capable hands. The Trustees are appointed by H.R.H. the Prince of Wales, and the work of administration is being carried out by a Council also appointed by him.

It is significant that much of the finest service in aid of the Trust has come from some of the most hard-hit areas in the country. It is the mothers and fathers of poor boys and girls who know so well how much the work to which the Trust is devoted will mean in terms of health and opportunity.

But the task is a national one and one in which every class in the community has a share. King George's Jubilee Trust is not a charity: it is a permanent Thank-offering, which, through Their Majesties' own constant care for our country, takes this generous and noble form. In his message to his peoples on Jubilee Day, His Majesty dwelt on the importance of the work of the Trust. "It is to the young," he said, "that the future belongs."

H.R.H. the Prince of Wales, in his broadcast address to the Nation on the 12th of April, 1935, said: "I feel sure that the welfare of the rising generation will appeal to you all, and that everyone will wish to have their share in this Jubilee tribute to the King . . . Help me in building up this King George's Jubilee Trust on a national basis, in order to make it adequate not only to the object which it hopes to achieve but also to the occasion which it will serve to commemorate."

Those who wish to take a share in this National Thank-offering may send donations to: King George's Jubilee Trust, St. James's Palace, London, S.W.1.

Published by King George's Jubilee Trust, St. James's Palace, London, S.W.1.
Printed in England by Odhams Press Ltd., Long Acre, London, W.C.2.